Healthy Smoothie Recipes Healthy Herbal Smoothies That Are Nutritious, Delicious and Easy to Make

Healthy Smoothies Made With Herbs and Spices

by:
Lee Anne Dobbins

Table Of Contents

Introduction

Chances are that you're already familiar with smoothies and you know that they can be a healthy snack or meal alternative. Most smoothies are made with various combinations of fruit and yogurt and some even have vegetables. They taste great, are easy to make, and give you a lot of vitamins in a small package.

What you probably don't know is that you can add a healthy wallop to those smoothies by incorporating herbs and spices into them! That's because herbs and spices offer a concentration of all kinds of nutrients and healthy compounds for your body. Adding herbs and spices to your smoothies can also enhance the flavor, just like they enhance the flavor of your food.

Various herbs and spices have been used since ancient times to cure a host of ailments and prevent illness. They offer much more than just vitamins and minerals, herbs and spices have compounds that address specific health problems and work to alleviate them. Adding these herbs and spices to your smoothies can be a fun and flavorful way of addressing health issues you may be having as well as helping to prevent future health problems.

With all these great advantages, there's no reason NOT to add herbs and spices to your smoothies! In this book, I have included 35 of my favorite healthy herbal smoothies that use common herbs and spices (ones you probably already have in your kitchen) and are easy to make and delicious to drink.

Why Drink Smoothies?

Health professionals recommend that you get 9 servings of fruits and vegetables a day - that's 9 cups! This isn't some arbitrary number either, this is the amount of fruits and vegetables that experts feel will give you the best chance of getting enough of the vitamins and minerals that our bodies need to function.

Needless to say, it can be pretty difficult to work 9 cups of fruits and veggies into your day - most of us get a cup or two if we are lucky. Thankfully, there is an easy way to get the recommended amount and that is by incorporating them into smoothies!

Smoothies allow you to blend together your fruits and vegetables into a smaller space. 2 cups of fruit might end up being 1 cup of smoothie, but it still has all the same healthy vitamins and minerals. The biggest difference though is that because you are mixing your fruits and vegetables with other ingredients, you are making a tasty treat that feels more like a dessert than something you "have to eat because it is good for you". This is a perfect way to get kids to eat their recommended daily amount of fruits and vegetables too!

The other benefit to smoothies, especially when it comes to vegetables is that you are eating the veggies raw instead of cooked. Cooking vegetables takes out some of the vital nutrients so eating them raw is great for your health. Another benefit is that there are no messy pots and pans to clean up. In fact, there is very little cleanup involved with making smoothies - you don't have any mixing bowls, pots or pans and, depending on what you are adding, you may not even need to cut anything up so you might not even need a knife or cutting board! Just put your ingredients in the blender and blend! Once you are done, you can simply put some water with a drop of dish detergent in the blender and turn it on for a few seconds to clean it. Then just rinse the soap out and you're ready for your next smoothie.

Smoothies not only allow you to get your daily allotment of fruits and vegetables, but you can work in other healthy foods like flax seed, coconut oil, kefir, healthy algae and, as this book shows you, herbs and spices. In short, if you put the right ingredients in your smoothies, they can be like little powerhouses of health and vitality giving you increased energy and filling you with nutrients for the day.

When compared with juicing, smoothies have a distinct advantage due to the fact that juicing removes the fiber from the fruits or vegetables. Smoothies contain all the fiber because you are grinding up the whole fruit and not extracting the pulp like a juicer does. As you know, fiber is an important part of your diet - it helps keep your system regular and is important for heart health too. Most people don't get nearly enough fiber so smoothies are a great way to get more of it without even realizing that you are!

Another thing you can do is turn smoothies into a complete meal by adding protein. Adding something like egg whites (either from eggs or the egg whites that you get in the container) will add protein but not affect the taste. You could also add protein powder which, depending on the flavor of the powder, might add to the taste. I don't have any of those recipes in this book, but you could add 1/2 a cup of egg whites or a scoop of powder to most of these recipes without affecting the taste too drastically.

How To Make A Smoothie

A smoothie is just a liquid blend of fruits, vegetables and other ingredients. You can literally put anything in your smoothie that you want. Their are no rules about smoothies and the combinations and opportunities for creating new recipes are endless.

That being said, there are some general guidelines you should follow.

First of all, you want your smoothie to be cold. The colder the better as far as I am concerned. In order to achieve this, I usually add ice cubes to the drink. If you think the ice cubes "water it down" too much, then you could opt for frozen fruit. I usually keep a bag of frozen blueberries and raspberries in the freezer along with some bananas that I have cut in half (without the peels) to use in smoothies.

You'll probably also want a bit of liquid in your smoothie to get it "drinkable". You can use anything you want - water, fruit juice, milk. A healthy alternative to milk is to use soy milk, almond milk or coconut milk. You could even use coconut water either from a can or straight from the coconut. In some of the recipes in this book you will see that I use coconut milk, but if you don't like the coconut taste you can substitute almond milk or even regular milk.

You can mix any kind of fruits or vegetables together that you want. At first it might seem a little strange to mix fruits with vegetables in a smoothie but some of them go very nicely together - try it and you might find you really like it!

Also, don't be afraid to add in different herbs and spices like I have in the recipes in this book, they add healthy flavor to the drink and boost the vitamin and mineral content of your smoothie.

Here's the steps you can use to make your own smoothies:

1. Add a liquid. For two servings, I usually use about 1/2 cup of some sort of liquid. As stated above this could be water, almond milk, juice etc.... If you are using fruits that are very juicy, like watermelon or oranges, you probably don't need to add any liquid.

2. Add ice or frozen fruit.

3. Add yogurt if you are including it in your smoothie.
4. Add your fruits and veggies (whatever combination you have come up with - don't be afraid to experiment).

5. Add sweetener if you want - If I think the smoothie needs some added sweetening, I usually add honey for a sweetener.

6. Add flavorings and spices. You can add in vanilla extract or any flavored extract or spices like cinnamon or herbs like ginger or rosemary for added flavor.

7. Blend the smoothie - start off with your blender (I use a Vitamix) on low and then gradually increase the speed. Let it run for a minute or so until blended.

Making smoothies can be a fun and creative process. This book includes some of my favorite recipes but don't be afraid to come up with some food combinations of your own to create delicious healthy smoothies that your family will love!

Smoothie Recipes

Sage Banana Pineapple Smoothie

This is very smooth with a little savory bite at the end from the sage. Sage has been known for ages as an overall tonic for good health. It contains an abundance of volatile oils and flavinoids and is a powerful anti inflammatory. Pineapple also has anti inflammatory properties so this is a good smoothie to help reduce problems from inflammatory conditions like arthritis and asthma.

Makes 2 servings

Ingredients:

7 ice cubes
1 banana, peeled
1 cup non fat greek yogurt
1 tablespoon honey
1 cup pineapple
1/2 tablespoon chopped sage

Combine all ingredients in a high powered blender and blend on high until they are well mixed.

Nutritional Value:
Per Serving: 272 calories, 51 g carbohydrates, 7g fat, 5g protein

Strawberry Banana Pineapple Basil Smoothie

This smoothie has a ton of vitamin C from the strawberries and pineapple. The basil has powerful anti-inflammatory and anti bacterial properties as well as vitamins and minerals. Basil has been used as a relaxing herb for centuries, so sit back and relax while you sip this healthy smoothie.

Makes 2 servings

Ingredients:

7 ice cubes
1 banana, peeled
1 cup non fat greek yogurt
1 tablespoon honey
1/2 cup pineapple
1/2 cup strawberries
1/2 tablespoon chopped fresh basil

Combine all ingredients in a high powered blender and blend on high until they are well mixed.

Nutritional Value:

Per Serving: 263 calories, 48g carbohydrates, 7g fat, 6g protein

Rosemary Pear Ginger Smoothie

Rosemary is a potent and delicious herb used mostly in meat dishes but it can go great with fruits too! Rosemary has been used for thousands of years to relieve nervousness, and enhance memory. It is a powerful antiseptic, anti-depressant, antiviral and anti-inflammatory herb. It has also been used historically to help soothe nausea as has ginger which is also included in this smoothie, so it's a great one to drink if you have an upset stomach.

Makes 2 servings

Ingredients:

7 ice cubes
1 banana, peeled
1 pear, with skin, seeds removed
3/4 cup coconut milk
3/4 teaspoon fresh ginger, grated
1/2 teaspoon fresh rosemary chopped

Combine all ingredients in a high powered blender and blend on high until they are well mixed.

Nutritional Value:

Per Serving: 121 calories, 31g carbohydrates, 3g fat, 2g protein

Apple Pear Ginger Turmeric Smoothie

Turmeric may be one of the most beneficial spices for your health. It is currently being studied extensively for its role in helping to treat and prevent cancer as well as its possible role in helping to relive the pain of arthritis. Since ancient times, its been used to treat colic, toothaches, menstrual problems and flatulence. In order for your body to absorb all the health benefits of turmeric, you should make sure you eat it with fat (in this case the coconut oil) and black pepper (sprinkle it on the top of the smoothie).

Makes 2 servings

Ingredients:

7 ice cubes
1 banana, peeled
1 pear, seeds removed (leave the skin on)
1 apple, seeds removed (leave the skin on)
3/4 cup coconut milk
1/2 teaspoon coconut oil
3/4 teaspoon ginger
1/8 teaspoon turmeric
Freshly ground black pepper

Combine all ingredients in a high powered blender and blend on high until they are well mixed. Give a couple of twists of the pepper mill over the smoothie after you pour it in the glass, it will give the smoothie a little zing and help your body absorb the nutrients from the turmeric.

Nutritional Value:

Per Serving: 350 calories, 81g carbohydrates, 9g fat, 3g protein

Strawberry Pineapple Basil

In addition to being a powerful antibacterial and anti-inflammatory herb, basil also has Vitamin K, Vitamin A, Vitamin C, potassium, magnesium, iron and calcium. Strawberries and pineapple also have Vitamin C, Vitamin A, potassium and other vitamins and minerals making this a heathy and tasty smoothie. The basil adds a refreshing coolness to this drink.

Makes 2 servings

Ingredients:

7 ice cubes
1 cup strawberries
1 cup pineapple
1 1/2 tablespoon fresh basil ,chopped

Combine all ingredients in a high powered blender and blend on high until they are well mixed.

Nutritional Value:

Per Serving: 62 calories, 16g carbohydrates, 0g fat, 1g protein

Mango Banana Ginger

This smoothie features two tasty and healing herbs - ginger and cinnamon. Used to help with digestion and regulate blood sugar, they make a perfect compliment to the banana and mango giving the drink a spicy tropical flair.

Makes 2 servings

Ingredients:

7 ice cubes
1 mango, cored and chopped
1 banana
1/2 cup coconut milk
1/4 tablespoon fresh ginger
1/4 teaspoon cinnamon

Combine all ingredients in a high powered blender and blend on high until they are well mixed.

Nutritional Value:

Per Serving: 150 calories, 35g carbohydrates, 2g fat, 2g protein

Pineapple Strawberry Banana Turmeric

This is another smoothie that has one of the healthiest spices - turmeric - in it. Turmeric has a lot of health benefits, not the least of which is that experts feel it may play a role in preventing many types of cancer. It should be taken with a fat and some black pepper for maximum effectiveness so I've included some coconut oil as the fat and a few twists of the pepper mill into your glass will add some spice to the taste of the smoothie without "ruining" it.

Makes 2 servings

Ingredients:

7 ice cubes
1 cup strawberries
1 cup pineapple
1 banana
1/4 teaspoon turmeric
1/2 tablespoon coconut oil
1/2 teaspoon vanilla extract

Put all the ingredients in your blender and blend on high for about two minutes until all ingredients are mixed. The coconut oil helps you absorb the nutrients from the turmeric. After you pour the smoothie into your glass, put a couple twists from the pepper mill in the glass as the pepper also helps absorb nutrients.

Nutritional Value:

Per Serving: 159 calories, 32g carbohydrates, 4g fat, 2g protein

Frozen Berry Basil Smoothie

I always keep a stockpile of frozen fruits in my freezer so I can whip up an icy cold smoothie any time I want. Although you might think of basil as just something that goes in Italian food, it actually is a good compliment to fruit smoothies because it has a licorice - minty flavor. Both berries and basil are loaded with healthy anti-oxidants and this smoothie only has 154 calories per serving so drink up!

Makes 2 servings

Ingredients:

2 cups coconut milk
1 cup frozen blueberries
1 cup frozen raspberries
4 fresh basil leaves chopped
1/4 teaspoon vanilla

Put all the ingredients in your blender and blend on high. Because of all the frozen berries, you can eat this with a spoon - if you want it to be more liquid just add more coconut milk or wait a bit before eating to give it time to "melt".

Nutritional Value:

Per Serving: 154 calories, 25g carbohydrates, 5g fat, 3g protein

Mango Pear Ginger Turmeric - Cancer Fighting Smoothie

I love the combination of mango and pear with the ginger and turmeric. Kind of smooth, spicy and woody all at once. This is an unusually delicious and healthy smoothie. Both turmeric and ginger are thought to be able to aid in cancer prevention and ginger can also help with nausea, headaches and fighting off colds. Turmeric can help as a liver detoxifier, is a natural pain killer and can also help boost the effects of the chemotherapy drug paclitaxel as well as reduce the side effects.

Makes 2 servings

Ingredients:

7 ice cubes
1 mango, cored
1 pear, seeds removed
1/2 cup coconut milk
1/4 teaspoon coconut oil
1/4 tablespoon ginger, grated
1/4 teaspoon turmeric

Mix all ingredients in a blender on high until smooth. To help absorb the healthy nutrients from the turmeric, add some freshly ground black pepper to the top of your smoothie.

Nutritional Value:

Per Serving: 122 calories, 33g carbohydrates, 3g fat, 2g protein

Pineapple Banana Mint

Mint has ben used for centuries, not only for it's pleasing taste, but also for it's powerful medicinal properties. It is well known as an aid for digestion and can also help with nausea, headaches, respiratory problems and oral care. It's loaded with Vitamin A, Vitamin C, Vitamin B12, riboflavine, thiamin and folic acid.

Makes 2 servings

Ingredients:

7 ice cubes
1 cup pineapple
1 banana, peeled
1 cup coconut milk
2 tablespoons fresh mint

Put all the ingredients in a blender and mix until well blended. This one doesn't come out as thick as some of the others, if you prefer it thicker, you could freeze the pineapple and banana ahead of time or add less coconut milk.

Nutritional Value:

Per Serving: 141 calories, 29g carbohydrates, 3g fat, 2g protein

Strawberry Cucumber With Mint

Cucumber and strawberries?   Believe it or not, cucumber adds a fresh, crisp taste to any smoothie and goes pretty good with strawberries and other fruits too.   The mint adds antioxidant vitamins and minerals and has antibacterial and anti fungal properties.

Makes 2 servings

Ingredients:

1 cup cucumber
1 cup strawberries
1/2 cup non fat greek yogurt, plain
1 tablespoon honey
1 tablespoon chopped fresh mint

Put all the ingredients in a blender and mix in high until well blended. This one comes out a little tart, if you want it sweeter you could add more honey and more mint (or maybe even a banana) but if you like tart then you will love it the way it is!

Nutritional Value:

Per Serving: 100 calories, 19g carbohydrates, 0g fat, 7g protein

Scarborough Fair Smoothie

I couldn't resist naming this the "Scarborough Fair" smoothie after the song because it contains parsley, sage, rosemary and thyme. That might sound a bit herby for a smoothie but it actually is very tasty and loaded with antioxidants and vitamins (especially vitamin K). A super healthy and very low calorie smoothie that is savory instead of sweet. The avocado adds a little bit of creaminess and is also very good for you, especially when it comes to heart health.

Makes 2 servings

Ingredients:

2 cups fresh parsley
1 tablespoon fresh sage
1/2 teaspoon fresh rosemary
1/2 tablespoon fresh thyme
1 1/2 cups carrots (I chop them up so they blend easier)
3 celery stalks (including leaves)
1/4 cup avocado
7 ice cubes
1 cup water

Put all ingredients in the blender and mix on high for 1 to 2 minutes until it is all blended. This smoothie has a very mild taste with a herby after taste.

Nutritional Value:

Per Serving: 109 calories, 12g carbohydrates, 3g fat, 2g protein

Orange Creamsicle Smoothie

This is one of my favorites and it really does taste like an orange creamsicle! The cinnamon can help lower cholesterol, keep blood from being too sticky, relieve headaches and even help boost memory. Vanilla can aid in weight loss and help reduce anxiety. As with most herbs and spices, both are loaded with antioxidants as are the oranges.

Makes 2 servings

Ingredients:

7 ice cubes
2 oranges (peeled)
1 cup vanilla flavored nonfat greek yogurt
1/2 teaspoon vanilla extract
1/2 teaspoon cinnamon

Put all the ingredients into the blender and blend at high speed until they are mixed.

Nutritional Value:

Per Serving: 158 calories, 28g carbohydrates, 0g fat, 13g protein

Drink Your Salad Smoothie

Don't like eating salads? Then why not drink them?
You're supposed to have at least one a day but if
you're like me and can only seem to eat a little bit
before you get bored, then putting the ingredients
into a smoothie is a great idea. It tastes surprisingly
good and is loaded with all the fiber, vitamins and
minerals you get from eating a salad.

Makes 2 servings

Ingredients:

7 ice cubes
1/2 cup water (or v8 juice)
1 tomato
2 celery stalks
1 cucumber
1 cup spinach leaves or mixed greens
1 tablespoon onion
1 teaspoon chives
1/2 cup avocado

Put all the ingredients into a blender and blend until
mixed well. If you want a spicier version you can
use spicy v8 juice instead of water or add in some
jalapenos.

Nutritional Value:

Per Serving: 100 calories, 10g carbohydrates, 6g fat, 3g protein

Pizza Smoothie

This one will remind you of pizza - well, without the bread and cheese of course! But it's much better for you than a pizza and it has hardly any calories! The basil, oregano and parsley have a host of healthy vitamins and other nutrients. The garlic can help regulate blood pressure and cholesterol levels and is a powerful natural antibiotic.

Makes 2 servings

Ingredients:

7 ice cubes
1 tomato
1 clove garlic (I mince it so that it gets distributed evenly)
1 cup water or v8 juice
2 stalks celery
1 tablespoon fresh basil
1/2 cup fresh parsley
1/2 teaspoon fresh oregano
1/4 teaspoon red pepper flakes (optional)
salt and pepper to taste

Put everything in the blender and mix for 1 to 2 minutes until well blended.

Nutritional Value:

Per Serving: 27 calories, 5g carbohydrates, 0g fat,
1g protein

Hot and Spicy Weight Loss Smoothie

I call this a weight loss smoothie because it is so low in calories that your body will probably burn them all off by digesting it. Not only that but the spicy taste will help curb any cravings you have and the cayenne pepper will raise your metabolism. Of course, it's loaded with vitamins and anti-oxidants too. Like it spicer? Just add more cayenne pepper to the recipe!

Makes 1 large serving

Ingredients:

7 ice cubes
1 large tomato
1 clove garlic
2 stalks celery
1/4 teaspoon cayenne pepper

Add all the ingredients to the blender and mix for 1 minute or until thoroughly blended.

Nutritional Value:

Per Serving: 55 calories, 12g carbohydrates, 0g fat, 3g protein

Sweet and Salty Smoothie

This is an unlikely combination that tastes great! Pineapple and celery are great anti-inflammatory foods loaded with vitamins and celery can help regulate blood pressure and is an effective diuretic.

Makes 2 servings

Ingredients:

7 ice cubes
3 cups fresh pineapple
5 stalks celery

Add all the ingredients to the blender and mix on high until well blended. A nice variation for this would be to freeze the pineapple and then omit the ice cubes. It would be thicker and more flavorful. Also, you can adjust the saltiness by adding more or less celery.

Nutritional Value:

Per Serving: 133 calories, 34g carbohydrates, 1g fat, 3g protein

Anti Inflammatory Smoothie

This smoothie contains some of the top anti-inflammatory fruits and spices as well as green tea which is well known for it's healthy and anti inflammatory properties. Eating anti-inflammatory foods is important for your health because inflammation is the start of most disease.

Makes 2 servings

Ingredients:

7 ice cubes
1 cup pineapple
1 cup papaya
1/2 cup green tea (cold)
1/4 teaspoon turmeric
1 tablespoon fresh basil leaves, chopped
1/2 teaspoon cinnamon
1/2 teaspoon fresh ginger, grated

Combine all ingredients in blender and blend well on high.

Nutritional Value:

Per Serving: 69 calories, 18g carbohydrates, 0g fat, 1g protein

Vitamin C Smoothie

This one is loaded with foods high in vitamin C. Of course, they have other vitamins and minerals as well as taste delicious together. The parsley is a great health tonic herb which is also high in Vitamin K and folate for good heart health.

Makes 2 servings

Ingredients:

7 ice cubes
1 kiwi, peeled
1 cup papaya
2 oranges
1/2 cup pineapple
1/2 cup strawberries
1/4 cup fresh parsley

Combine all ingredients in a blender and blend on high until smooth (about 1 minute). As an alternative, you could freeze all the fruits the night before and then omit the ice cubes.

Nutritional Value:

Per Serving: 195 calories, 49g carbohydrates, 1g fat, 5g protein

Pina Colada Smoothie

Coconut and pineapple make a great flavor combination and the fresh ginger helps to boost your immune system and is a powerful anti-inflammatory herb.

Makes 2 servings

Ingredients:

7 ice cubes
1/2 cup coconut milk
1 small apple, cored but leave skin on
1 cup pineapple
1 banana
1/2 teaspoon fresh ginger, grated

Add all ingredients to a blender and blend on high power until everything is mixed. If you prefer more of a coconut flavor, you could add some coconut extract, just about 1/4 teaspoon should be enough.

Nutritional Value:

Per Serving: 138 calories, 33g carbohydrates, 2g fat, 2g protein

Cardamom Mango Smoothie

Cardamom is not one of the popular herbs that you hear about all the time so I wanted to find a smoothie that would showcase it's taste and here it is! Cardamom is an important spice in Ayurvedic healing - it is a good stimulant, helps with stomach issues and can be useful in treating seasonal allergies and sore throat.

Makes 2 servings

Ingredients:

7 ice cubes
1 cup lowfat vanilla greek yogurt
1 cup mango
1/2 cup coconut water
1/4 teaspoon cardamom

Put everything in the blender and blend on high until well mixed. You can use canned coconut water, or tap a coconut and drain the water and use that!

Nutritional Value:

Per Serving: 173 calories, 33g carbohydrates, 2g fat, 10g protein

Stomach Soothing Smoothie

This smoothie has all the natural ingredients that help soothe an upset stomach - ginger, banana and peppermint have all been known for ages as stomach soothing foods and combining them in this delicious drink is a great way to get rid of an upset stomach.

Makes 1 serving

Ingredients:

7 ice cubes
1 banana
1 cup water
1" ginger root, grated
1 tablespoon fresh peppermint

Combine all ingredients in blender and blend on high until well mixed.

Nutritional Value:

Per Serving: 131 calories, 33g carbohydrates, 0g fat, 1g protein

Carrot Apple Smoothie

Get your fruits and veggies all in one sitting with this delicious smoothie loaded with Vitamin A and the health benefits of cinnamon and nutmeg which include lowering blood pressure, regulating blood sugar, enhancing cognitive function, relieving indigestion and liver and kidney detoxification.

Makes 2 small servings or 1 large

Ingredients:

7 ice cubes
1 apple, cored and seeded (leave skin on)
1 cup grated carrots
1/2 cup apple juice
1/2 teaspoon cinnamon
1/8 teaspoon nutmeg

Combine all ingredients in blender and blend on high. If you want a creamier version, add 1/2 cup yogurt and 1 teaspoon honey.

Nutritional Value:

Per Serving (1/2 of the recipe): 98 calories, 25g carbohydrates, 0g fat, 1g protein

Pumpkin Pie Smoothie

This smoothie evokes memories of delicious holiday pies, but you don't have to wait until the holidays to whip one up, in fact, you'll want to make this all year round because it's delicious and loaded with health benefits. The pumpkin is a powerhouse food with low calories, lots of fiber and a ton of Vitamin A, Vitamin C and Vitamin E as well as various minerals. Cinnamon can help with memory and brain function as well as help regulate blood sugar and lower cholesterol and also has antioxidants and vitamins. Allspice has vitamins, minerals and anti-inflammatory properties.

Makes 2 servings

Ingredients:

7 ice cubes
1 cup canned pumpkin
1/2 cup plain nonfat greek yogurt
1/2 cup skim milk
2 tablespoons maple syrup
1 teaspoon vanilla extract
1/8 teaspoon allspice
1/8 teaspoon cinnamon
pinch nutmeg

Put all the ingredients in a blender and mix until smooth.

Nutritional Value:

Per Serving: 157 calories, 29g carbohydrates, 1g fat, 11g protein

Anise Green Smoothie

This green smoothie includes spinach and cilantro, which are good sources of vitamin K. They are also rich in vitamins and minerals as well as antioxidants. The smoothie is sweetened with pineapple and mango along with the spice anise which has antimicrobial properties and can be used to relieve digestive problems.

Makes 1 large serving

Ingredients:

7 ice cubes
1/2 cup pineapple
1/2 cup mango
1/2 cup fresh cilantro
1/2 cup fresh spinach
1/2 teaspoon ground anise

Add all the ingredients to the blender and blend on high speed until well mixed - about 1 minute.

Nutritional Value:

Per Serving: 118 calories, 26g carbohydrates, 0g fat, 4g protein

Vitamin K Smoothie

1/2 cup of kale has 500% times the USRDA of vitamin K (plus 150% of vitamin A) and 1/2 cup of parsley also has 500% of the USRDA of vitamin K as well as a host of other vitamins and minerals. Vitamin K is important for heart health and can help reduce blood clotting (if you are on drugs for this already, you might want to forgo this smoothie).

Makes 2 servings

Ingredients:

7 ice cubes
1 cup kale
1/2 cup parsley
1/2 bartlett pear
1/2 cup green grapes
1 banana
1 cup watermelon

Put all ingredients in the blender and blend in high for 1 or 2 minutes until blended. The grapes, banana and watermelon will cut through the bitter taste of the greens so if you prefer more sweetness just add more of those!

Nutritional Value:

Per Serving: 123 calories, 35g carbohydrates, 0g fat, 3g protein

Vitamin A Smoothie

This smoothie is loaded with fruits and vegetables that are high in Vitamin A. Vitamin A is responsible for good eye health, keeping your mucus membranes and skin healthy, maintaining healthy bones and teeth, and fighting diseases caused by viruses.

Makes 2 servings

Ingredients:

7 ice cubes
1 cup cantaloupe
1 cup mango
1/2 cup carrots
1/2 teaspoon paprika

Add all the ingredients to the blender and mix on high until well blended. If you want a more dense fruit flavor, freeze the fruit ahead of time and omit the ice cubes. Paprika is very high in vitamin A, but the amount can be lessened or eliminated if you don't like the spicy zing it gives to this smoothie.

Nutritional Value:

Per Serving: 98 calories, 26g carbohydrates, 0g fat, 2g protein

Sore Throat Smoothie

This smoothie has a variety of herbs and foods that are known to help soothe sore throats. These foods also contain vitamins and nutrients that help fight the colds that cause sore throats.

Makes 1 serving

Ingredients:

4 ice cubes
1/2 teaspoon fresh grated ginger
1/2 lemon, peeled
1 orange, peeled
1 clove garlic
1/2 cup vanilla flavored greek yogurt
1 tablespoon honey

Mix all ingredients in blender until smooth.

Nutritional Value:

Per Serving: 230 calories, 50g carbohydrates, 0g fat, 10g protein

Blood Pressure Reducer Smoothie

This smoothie includes all kinds of herbs and foods that are known to help reduce blood pressure. Celery helps relax the artery walls and enable better blood flow, dandelion is a natural diuretic that releases excess sodium without releasing potassium, raspberries have fiber, vitamin C and potassium - all of which help lower blood pressure. Bananas are a rich source of potassium. Low fat dairy has lots of calcium and magnesium, all of which play a role in healthy blood pressure. Spinach and coriander are high in magnesium.

Makes 2 servings

Ingredients:

7 ice cubes
1 celery stalk
1/2 cup dandelion leaves
1/2 cup raspberries
1 banana, peeled
1/2 cup low fat greek yogurt
1/2 cup spinach
1 cup watermelon
1/8 teaspoon coriander

Put the ingredients in a high powered blender and mix on high until well blended.

Nutritional Value:

Per Serving: 230 calories, 50g carbohydrates, 0g fat, 10g protein

Blood Sugar Regulating Smoothie

Keeping your blood sugar on an even keel is important for your overall health. If your blood sugar gets too low, you can end up getting cravings and overeating. For diabetics in particular, eating foods that keep blood sugar stable, like the foods in this smoothie, should be a daily goal.

Makes 2 servings

Ingredients:

7 ice cubes
1 apple, cored and seeded but with skin still on
1 pear, cored and seeded but with skin still on
1 tablespoon cinnamon
1 cup low fat greek yogurt

Put all ingredients in blender and mix on high until well blended.

Nutritional Value:

Per Serving: 200 calories, 39g carbohydrates, 3g fat, 12g protein

Mood Boosting Smoothie

This smoothie contains foods and herbs known to improve your mood. A tasty drink that is sure to pick you up when you feel a little down in the dumps!

Makes 1 serving

Ingredients:

7 ice cubes
The zest of 1 lemon
The juice of 1 lemon
1 cup nonfat greek yogurt
1/2 tablespoon cinnamon
1 tablespoon honey
1/2 teaspoon vanilla extract

Put all the ingredients in the blender and mix on high until well blended. If you want it sweeter, add more honey and vanilla. For creamier add more yogurt. You can play around with the ingredients as you see fit, the ratio of amounts do not effect the effectiveness of the smoothie.

Nutritional Value:

Per Serving: 221 calories, 34g carbohydrates, 0g fat, 23g protein

Memory Enhancing Smoothie

Rosemary has many health benefits but it's beneficial effect on memory is due to the presence of carnosic acid which is neuroprotective and helps with memory retention. One study showed that even simply smelling rosemary could improve the memories of office workers. Sage helps break down acetylcholine which your brain needs to function properly. Yogurt has protein that your brain needs to remain alert. I've combined all of these and more foods that help memory function into this delicious "memory enhancing" smoothie.

Makes 2 servings

Ingredients:

7 ice cubes
1 cup red grapes
1/2 cup blueberries
1 apple, cored and seeds removed (leave the skin on)
1/2 cup spinach
1/2 cup green tea
1/2 cup nonfat greek yogurt
1/2 teaspoon fresh rosemary
1 teaspoon fresh sage

Put all ingredients in a blender and blend on high until fully mixed.

Nutritional Value:

Per Serving: 147 calories, 33g carbohydrates, 0g fat, 7g protein

Anti Aging Smoothie

This smoothie contains some of the most powerful anti-aging herbs. Ginger and turmeric are loaded with vitamins and minerals as well as nutrients that help with age related illness and problems like failing vision, memory loss and decreased immune function. Blueberries are loaded with nutrients that are known to help repair damaged tissue and improve memory.   Avocado has vitamin E, potassium and folates that help your skin look great and contribute to heart health.

Makes 2 servings

Ingredients:

7 ice cubes
1 cup coconut milk
1/2 cup blueberries
1/2 cup avocado
1/2 cup raspberries
1 cup pineapple
1 teaspoon fresh ginger, grated
1/2 teaspoon turmeric

Add all the ingredients to a blender and mix on high until they are well blended.

Nutritional Value:

Per Serving: 147 calories, 33g carbohydrates, 0g fat, 7g protein

Apple Pie Smoothie

You won't believe how much this taste like a real apple pie! My husband likes it sweet so I have listed the ingredients that he likes, but if it is too sweet for you, you can add less maple syrup and cinnamon. It's delicious and healthy and a lot less calories than a piece of apple pie (and easier to make too!)

Makes 3 servings

Ingredients:

7 ice cubes
2 apples, cored (leave the skin on, thats where a lot of the vitamins are)
1 cup plain nonfat greek yogurt
2 tablespoons maple syrup
1/4 teaspoon nutmeg
2 teaspoons cinnamon

Add all the ingredients to a blender and blend on high until well mixed.

Nutritional Value:

Per Serving: 238 calories, 50g carbohydrates, 1g fat, 12g protein

Pear and Apple Smoothie

The pears and apples in this smoothie compliment the cinnamon and turmeric perfectly making it a refreshing and healthy treat. As mentioned previously in this book, cinnamon has a host of health benefits and turmeric is extremely potent as an overall healing spice.

Makes 2 servings

Ingredients:

7 ice cubes
2 apples, cored and seeded (leave skin on)
2 pears with seeds removed but skin on
1 teaspoon cinnamon
1/4 teaspoon turmeric

Put all ingredients in blender and mix on high until smooth. Possible additions to this smoothie include yogurt for a creamier version and vanilla extract for a little more flavor. Also if you are looking for more sweetness, maple syrup or honey could work well.

Nutritional Value:

Per Serving: 140 calories, 46g carbohydrates, 1g fat, 1g protein

Conclusion

Smoothies are a great way to increase the amount of vitamins and minerals you get each day and adding herbs and spices also adds in other nutrients that are vital to your health. Herbs and spices are like little nutritional powerhouses so even a small amount of them has a lot of healing power. Plus they make the smoothies taste even better!

If you have certain health problems, you can even design smoothies to have foods, herbs and spices that will treat those problems. It's much easier to ingest a large volume of these in a smoothie than to try to eat them as part of your meals. I've included some smoothies that help with general health issues in this book, but if you have a particular health issue that is not included here, you can research the types of foods and herbs that treat that problem and come up with a delicious smoothie just for you!

Experimenting with ingredients for your smoothies can be a lot of fun, don't be afraid to make your own healthy smoothie creations with your own favorite, herbs, spices, fruits and veggies.

If you want to learn more about how eating delicious food can improve your health and get more healthy recipes, check out the rest of my healing foods books:

Healing Herbs & Spices : Health Benefits of Popular Herbs & Spices Plus Over 70 Recipes To Use Them In

Mood Boosting Foods and Mood Boosting Recipes

Healing Desserts : Guilt Free Desserts Made Healthier With Healing Foods, Herbs and Spices

Anti-Aging Herbs : Top Anti Aging Foods And How To Improve Your Health With Recipes That Use Them

Growing Herbs Indoors : Your Guide To Growing Herbs In Containers For A Vibrant Indoor Herb Garden

Also, I would love to talk to you on my blog, facebook or twitter:

Blog - http://www.healingfoodscookbooks.com

Facebook - http://www.facebook.com/ healingfoodsbooks

Twitter - http://www.twitter.com/healingfoodscb

Made in the USA
Lexington, KY
31 March 2013